Original title:
On the Shores of Utopia

Copyright © 2025 Creative Arts Management OÜ
All rights reserved.

Author: Tobias Sterling
ISBN HARDBACK: 978-1-80581-562-4
ISBN PAPERBACK: 978-1-80581-089-6
ISBN EBOOK: 978-1-80581-562-4

Memorandum of Dreamt Destinies

In a land where dreams take flight,
Fish wear hats, a comical sight.
The sun winks with a golden smile,
And clouds dance around for a while.

Balloons float high in the sky,
While squirrels in tuxedos sigh.
The grass giggles under our feet,
As laughter makes the day complete.

Celestial Light on Aqua Horizons.

Beneath a sunset made of jelly,
We rode on turtles, quite the belly!
The moon grinned wide, with ice cream cones,
As mermaids sang in silly tones.

Stars wore glasses and danced in line,
While sandcastles held a fancy soiree.
The waves played tricks, they splashed with glee,
And crabs served tea beneath a tree.

Whispers of a New Horizon

Where giggles tickle the morning breeze,
And daisies sip tea with honeybees.
The wind tells tales of runaway socks,
As time skips ropes on sunny docks.

Echoes clamor as we canter,
A parade of ducks, a quirky banter.
With hats of fruit and shoes of pie,
We wave at clouds, flitting by.

Dreamscapes by the Water's Edge

The water's edge, a curious place,
Where tadpoles practice their ballet grace.
With jellybeans caught in the tide,
And surfboards waiting for a ride.

The daffodils wear polka-dot shoes,
Sharing jokes with the ocean blues.
A picnic spread with laughter on top,
As the seagulls join in with a hop.

Skies Painted with Dreams

A painter shrugs at the blue,
With brushes made from sticky goo.
He splatters clouds like cream on pie,
And laughs as seagulls aim and fly.

The sun is wearing shades so bright,
It sparkles like a disco light.
Fish frolic dressed in fancy shorts,
As crabs do salsa on the docks.

The Lure of Infinite Horizons

A sailor dreams of distant shores,
But finds his boat in endless chores.
He trips on ropes, and sings so loud,
  He's popular with every crowd.

With snacks of chips and grape juice,
He claims he sailed a mighty moose.
The horizon winks, a cheeky tease,
"Just go outside and feel the breeze!"

Guiding Stars in Quiet Waters

Stars giggle in their velvet skies,
While fish below are wearing ties.
They dance beneath a moonlight glow,
While frogs croak tunes that ebb and flow.

The ducks in boots parade along,
With outfits loud, they sing their song.
A gentle wave, a playful splash,
Makes all the critters stomp and thrash.

Tides of Tenderness and Awakening

The tides laugh softly, swaying slow,
As penguins waddle in a row.
They slip and slide on sandy beaches,
With tales of treasure that each one preaches.

At dawn, the jellyfish dance and twirl,
In bloom with colors, they twist and whirl.
A surfboard dog rides waves with glee,
While gulls shout, 'Hey, look at me!'

Echoing Laughter Beneath Serene Skies

Bubbles rise, and so do giggles,
As we tell tales that twist and wiggle.
Sunshine paints our funny faces,
While ice cream drips in wild races.

Seagulls squawk with humor bright,
As we chase shadows, what a sight!
A flip-flop flies, a dog does bark,
And we all laugh till it gets dark.

Buckets full of sand and dreams,
We build castles, or so it seems.
A wave crashes, our laughter swells,
As sand sticks to our funny shells.

Giggling until we can't breathe,
In this paradise, we dare to weave.
With jellyfish jokes and beach ball cheers,
We dance through our joyful years.

Tidal Dances of the Soul

The tides go in, the tides go out,
While we twirl round without a doubt.
Shells become shoes, oh what a sight,
As we slide in and out of daylight.

A crab does tango, a fish does sway,
While dolphins laugh and play all day.
With flip-flops flying like paper planes,
We waltz with waves and burst with rains.

Our hearts are light, our steps are free,
As we shimmy along the sea.
With every splash and every roar,
We find new tunes to dance and soar.

So let the saltwater find your soul,
For laughter's the ultimate goal.
With sandy feet and heads held high,
We dive into joy beneath the sky.

Shores of Endless Storytelling

Gather 'round, let's spin some tales,
Of pirate ships and friendly whales.
With every wave, a story's spun,
As we forget the setting sun.

Sandcastles built keep crumbling down,
But laughter rises, wearing the crown.
A sea breeze whispers each plot twist,
As we shout out, 'You get the gist!'

Flying kites, with laughter so grand,
While waves applaud our carefree band.
With every giggle, the stories grow,
Like bubbles that dance, they ebb and flow.

So share your dreams, your wildest schemes,
As the ocean waves catch our gleams.
With friends beside, let's craft and weave,
A tapestry of joy that won't leave.

Harmonies of An Unbroken Dream

In a land where laughter blooms,
The cows wear shades and dance with tunes,
The sun plays hide and seek at noon,
While flowers laugh with a comical swoon.

A squirrel sings in a high-pitched style,
While the trees gossip and giggle a while,
Clouds float by with a whimsical grin,
As the sky's jester invites the fun in.

Pioneers of a New Dawn

We ride on bikes made of fluffy dreams,
As grasshoppers join our joyful schemes,
With pies in pockets and hats askew,
We chart a course where nonsense is new.

A map of giggles, a compass of cheer,
Of marshmallow mountains and lemonade beer,
We dance while the sun drips ice cream delight,
Pioneers of laughter, we take flight!

The Dance of Floating Petals

Petals twirl in a silly spree,
With bees wearing ties, they buzz with glee,
A chorus of frogs adorns the brook,
Reciting Shakespeare, but only half the book.

Twirling hats atop noses so wide,
They prance like they've all taken a glide,
The petals giggle as they sway and spin,
In this whimsical waltz, where to begin?

Valleys of Light and Laughter

In valleys where shadows play tricks with smiles,
And rivers of joy flow for endless miles,
The clouds are painted in hues of bright pink,
While raccoons trade secrets over a drink.

The hills are alive with the sounds of jest,
As trees lean in to hear the best,
With whirling winds bringing taffy and cheer,
Here, full of folly, we banish our fear.

Dreams Cradled in Ocean's Hands

Seagulls in tuxedos stroll,
Chasing dreams of fishy roles.
Waves whisper jokes from afar,
While crabs hold a dance, oh so bizarre.

Sunsets paint the sky in glee,
As jellyfish float like they're on a spree.
A dolphin sings a tuneful song,
While pirates laugh, "We can't be wrong!"

Turtles race without a care,
Pretending they are flying through the air.
Sandcastles wear crowns made of shells,
Echoing laughter, as joy compels.

In this place where silliness reigns,
The ocean chuckles, forgets its pains.
So take a dip in this playful sea,
Where smiles abound, and spirits are free.

Where the Heart Sails Free

A squirrel captain sets the course,
With a crew of ants, a tiny force.
They hoist a flag of mismatched socks,
Sailing bravely past friendly rocks.

The wind declares, "Let's have some fun!"
As it tickles waves under the sun.
Fishes gather, forming a band,
Playing tunes, oh, isn't it grand?

Coconuts dance with hula skirts,
While the seaweed sings of playful flirts.
A treasure map, made out of cheese,
Leads to laughter, as it does tease.

So here we sail, on whimsy's foam,
Hearts beating loud, like we're at home.
With every splash, we share a smile,
On this wacky sea, we'll stay awhile.

Tranquility's Bounty on Open Waves

A pirate parrot tells tall tales,
Of rubber ducks and wind-filled sails.
The fish wear sunglasses, looking fine,
While sea turtles enjoy half-priced wine.

The sun lounges, bathing in fun,
While crabs debate who's number one.
Starfish act like they own the beach,
"Oh, look at me!" they joyfully screech.

Clouds are pirates, plundering air,
With a bounty of dreams, we all can share.
Giggling waves tickle our toes,
As morning laughter gently blows.

So join the frolic, let worries cease,
Together we bask in this quirky peace.
For here in this laughter-laden sea,
We find tranquility, wild and free.

The Journey of Sheltered Hearts

In teacups sailing on a breeze,
Two frogs are giggling, sipping leaves.
They dodge the waves like they're on a date,
While fish throw confetti to celebrate.

Their boat a shell, adorned with flair,
Sails through jellybean-filled air.
A crab DJ spins the tunes,
As ducks do the cha-cha under moons.

Every splash is a dance of delight,
As seahorses twirl through the night.
The ocean bursts with laughter and cheer,
As we embrace this journey dear.

Sailing onward, hearts joined as one,
In this joyful world where fun's never done.
So grab your friends, let's play our part,
In this quirky quest of sheltered hearts.

Echoes of an Ideal Realm

In a place where fish wear hats,
And turtles ride on rolling mats,
The sun is always made of cheese,
And laughter dances with the breeze.

Waves whisper jokes to sandy toes,
While umbrellas flutter like they know,
The secret to an endless cheer,
Is not to take life too serious, dear.

Seagulls gossip, share their news,
About a crab who wears bright shoes,
The surfboards are all jammed with cream,
And everyone wakes up with a dream.

So grab a floatie, join the show,
In this land where giggles flow,
We'll build our castles, laugh and play,
In an echo of joy every day.

Beyond the Tides of Tomorrow

In a world where candy grows on trees,
And jellyfish float like puffy bees,
The clocks forget to tick and chime,
And mermaids sing in perfect rhyme.

Turtles throw confetti at the moon,
While octopuses juggle to a tune,
The skies are painted with silly sighs,
And everyone's wearing oversized ties.

Fish in bowler hats parade in style,
As dolphins giggle and wink with guile,
Here laughter sparkles in the air,
And worries vanish without a care.

So take a plunge, embrace the fun,
Where dreams are bright as the morning sun,
In this place where silliness reigns,
And joy is found in playful chains.

A Vision in the Mist

In foggy lands where winks are free,
And unicorns sip on herbal tea,
The morning dew is made of spritz,
While kittens dance in fancy blitz.

Lemons giggle under cloudy skies,
As rainbows wear their funny ties,
The clouds play peek-a-boo all day,
With fluffy friends who love to play.

Squirrels wear capes and take to flight,
In this place where wrong feels right,
Bananas joke and apples prank,
While joyful hearts gather at the bank.

Come dream with me in this hazy space,
Where laughter sings its sweetest grace,
In a vision where smiles are bright,
And everything feels just right.

The Land Where Wishes Dance

In a land where wishes twist and twirl,
And every leaf is a dancing girl,
The rivers tickle the rocks with care,
While giggling breezes tousle your hair.

Butterflies here wear polka dots,
And caterpillars play hopscotch lots,
The flowers chuckle, whisper in bloom,
Creating a symphony in full room.

Pies float by on clouds of fluff,
While ducks argue who's the cutest puff,
In this realm of whimsical glee,
Every moment's a hilarious spree.

So join the dance, let your wishes fly,
In a world where fun never says goodbye,
With laughter weaving through the trees,
In the land where joy is always a breeze.

A Symphony of Sea and Sky

Clouds dance like jellybeans, so spry,
Waves slap the shore with a cheery sigh.
Seagulls play tag, squawking in delight,
While boats race each other in the warm sunlight.

With every splash, laughter does soar,
Frisbees fly high, oh what a galore!
Sandy smiles and sunburnt skin,
This seaside circus is where fun begins.

Finding Joy in Hidden Coves

In a nook where laughter bubbles like stew,
We find treasures larger than a shoe.
Crabs don top hats and strut on the sand,
While starfish gossip, all perfectly planned.

Sunscreen slips and giggles abound,
As sandcastles topple, but laughter's around.
Seashells whisper secrets of old,
While adventure awaits, bright and bold.

Sculpting Dreams Amidst the Waves

With a bucket of hopes and a pinch of salt,
We mold our wishes, not one will halt.
A sandy giraffe waves to a coconut tree,
As jellybeans float on the bright, bubbly sea.

Our dreams take form on this golden stage,
Each splash a chapter, each wave a page.
Dancing with dolphins, oh what a sight,
In the laughter of sunlight, all feels just right.

The Embrace of Unfurling Possibilities

Kites paint the sky in colors so wild,
While clowns juggle seashells, each one a child.
Laughter erupts like a frothy wave,
In the sun-drenched haven, we're all so brave.

Endless horizons invite us to play,
With ice cream mustaches, we seize the day.
Echoes of joy clash with the sea's song,
In this whimsical place, where we all belong.

The Elysian Sea's Embrace

The seagulls sing, they steal my fries,
A fish in shades of neon tries.
The waves parade their frothy foam,
A crab, my friend, has found a home.

With sun hats crooked, we bask and laugh,
While sunburns sneak, it's quite the gaffe.
A mermaid waves with glittered scales,
Her coffee's cold, but who needs tales?

Tides of Hope and Reverie

The snorkel gear is far too tight,
The fish just giggle, oh what a sight!
Sandcastles crumble with a plop,
My bucket's blue, but I think I'll stop.

The sun sets low, it beams so bright,
A seagull steals my snack outright.
We dance and twirl on shifting sands,
And write our names with silly hands.

Echoes of Harmonious Shores

The tide rolls in, it hums a tune,
A dolphin jumps, I call him Moon.
With jellyfish waltzing in delight,
I slip and slide, oh what a fright!

The shells all giggle, scattered wide,
While crabs conspire, they're full of pride.
We build a fortress made of dreams,
With snacks piled high, or so it seems.

Where Light Meets Lush Coasts

The palm trees sway like dancers bold,
While beach balls bounce, or so I'm told.
Sunburn's creeping, oh, what a bust,
A seagull snickers, it's quite a must.

We sip from coconuts, so divine,
While crabby critters sing in line.
It's a party here by the salty air,
With laughter loud, it's beyond compare.

Portraits of a Perfect Isle

In a place where coconuts dance,
Palm trees wear sunglasses, perchance.
Seagulls debate over a fish,
While tourists just dream and wish.

Laughter spills like buckets of sun,
Sandy feet blending, having fun.
Crabs hold court in clumsy attire,
While flip-flops play in the sand's choir.

The breeze tells tales of joy and cheer,
Where each hiccup draws in a peer.
Mermaids giggle at sailors' slips,
As waves give playful, salty quips.

So if you're lost, don't you fret,
Just follow the giggles; not a threat.
In this perfect isle of blissful glee,
The punchlines flow like the endless sea.

Beneath the Skies of Elysium

Where clouds wear hats and shift like breeze,
The sun plays peekaboo with trees.
Butterflies sing their silly song,
As daisies dance all day long.

Pigs in pink like high fashion models,
Cheese wheels roll like lazy oodles.
Frogs wear tuxedos, quite absurd,
Chirping jokes that seem unheard.

The moon hangs low, with a wink and grin,
Telling stars to let the fun begin.
Rain showers feel like tickles from above,
A whimsical place we're all dreaming of.

So grab a seat and stay awhile,
Dancing through clouds is always worthwhile.
For under these skies, laughter's the aim,
Elysium's joy is all the same.

The Dance of Sunlit Waters

Waves do the cha-cha along the shore,
Shells spin like disco balls, never a bore.
Dolphins leap with jokes up their fins,
While crabs tap dance, where the fun begins.

Fish wear sunglasses to block the rays,
Each splash a giggle in secret play.
Boats bob along, singing the blues,
With parrots chattering, spreading the news.

The sun is a jester in bright, bold gold,
Its laughter echoed in stories retold.
Every splash a punchline, bright and true,
Life on the waves is a vibrant view.

So let's join the dance, don't be shy,
With each wave's crest, let laughter fly.
In sunlit waters, joy has no end,
Where mirth and waves comfortably blend.

Cradled by the Infinite Blue

Above us is a canvas, splashed with laughs,
Clouds mold into creatures, their silly gaffs.
Fishes in bowties swim around,
While ocean spray giggles, a bubbly sound.

Wandering seashells tell tales so grand,
Of mermaids playing in their own band.
While seahorses prance in a jolly parade,
With treasures of laughter, never to fade.

In this realm where mischief is light,
Each breeze carries a joke, feeling just right.
As the sun dips low, it's a humorous glow,
A comedy show in a watery flow.

So float on dreams within this hue,
Where the sky and the sea play peekaboo.
Cradle your chuckles, let them fuse,
In the infinite blue, there's only fun to choose.

Sails of Ambition on Calm Seas

With dreams like vessels, we set out,
Chasing giggles that twist, then shout.
A parrot squawks a joke or two,
As we navigate skies so blue.

Winds whisper softly, a playful tease,
Fish wear sunglasses, lounging with ease.
Seagulls in bow ties dance on the waves,
While jellyfish watch from their stylish caves.

The anchor's a rubber duck on a spree,
We toast with coconut drinks, so carefree.
In this world of whimsy, we proudly sail,
The horizon's a collage, laughter's our trail.

Nautical maps drawn in crayon hues,
Charting paths for our silly muse.
With each wave that we jovially ride,
Adventure awaits on this hilarious tide.

In Search of the Tranquil Beyond

We wandered far where the silliness grows,
Hoping to find where the chuckle bug goes.
In temples of tickles, the air's pure delight,
Frogs dip their toes, preparing for night.

The horizon's a canvas smeared with bright cheer,
Where llamas wear hats, spreading smiles near.
A caravan of giggles sails by in a fleet,
As we trade sighs for grins, what a treat!

With each step, we find treasures of fun,
Mirthful delights, like a good pun won.
The tranquil beyond is a joyful parade,
A carnival of laughter we can't evade.

In this land where the odd always shines,
We dance through the gardens of vine-patterned lines.
So join us in revelry, come take a peek,
At the silliness thriving, splendidly unique.

Sunkissed Dreams and Starry Nights

Beneath the sun in a hammock swing,
We plot our schemes with each loopy fling.
Dreams dipped in syrup, sticky and sweet,
As we feast on laughter, a marvelous treat.

Stars twinkle down with a wink and a grin,
Jellybeans raining, where do we begin?
The moon's a disco ball, spinning around,
While crickets chirp tunes with their own funky sound.

Caught in this glow, we sway to the beat,
Giraffes join the dance, all nimble on feet.
Pillow fights happen as clouds float by,
The night whispers secrets, under the sky.

With sunburned laughs and sleepy goodbyes,
We drift in our dreams, beneath cosmic skies.
Sunkissed memories, forever in sight,
In the embrace of an all-star night.

The Heartbeat of Contentment

In a quirky little town where the clocks all unwind,
A cat runs the bakery, oh, what a find!
Let's feast on cookies shaped like old shoes,
And sip chocolate rivers while jiving to blues.

The grass tickles toes as we roll down the hills,
Where umbrellas blossom and laughter just spills.
We swing from the branches of dreaming big dreams,
Riding bicycles that play ukulele themes.

In full bloom of joy, we dance through the streets,
Followed by ants in their spectacles, neat.
The heartbeat of bliss keeps us all in sync,
As bubbles float by, we ponder and think.

So lift your glass high, toast to the days,
Where silliness reigns in whimsical ways.
Contentment's a puppy who licks every face,
In this carnival kingdom, we've found our place.

Reflections Under the Moonlit Canopy

Beneath the stars, we dance and prance,
In wobbly shoes, we take our chance.
The moonlight giggles at our silly moves,
As laughter echoes, and joy improves.

In laughter's grip, we twist and shout,
While squirrels join in, no jumble of doubt.
A bumblebee buzzes with rhythm and cheer,
Giggling softly, it draws near.

We toast to mischief with cups of lemonade,
To tales of fish that got away, and parades.
Amidst the glimmers of our youthful dreams,
Life's a laughing stock, or so it seems.

So come join us, under this shining dome,
Where absurdity reigns, and we feel at home.
With quirky nightcaps and sparkly eyes,
We dream of wild adventures in the skies.

Glistening Paths to Golden Dreams

With sprinkles of joy, we skip on the path,
Tracing our footsteps, avoiding the math.
The puddles reflect our goofy grins,
As we race past the fences, and elephant skins.

A pie in the sky, or a banana on top,
Who knew that laughter could never just stop?
With each little stumble, we cherish the fall,
As clowns at the circus, we answer the call.

Golden dreams shimmer, like soap on the lawn,
When frogs start to dance at the crack of dawn.
In a world of pink unicorns making us swoon,
Who needs a map? We'll just fly to the moon!

So we chase after giggles, on paths paved in cheer,
Skipping from here to the land of good beer.
In this whirligig journey, our hearts take flight,
As we twirl to the music of pure delight.

The Call of Serene Shores

With flip-flops flapping, we run to the beach,
A sandcastle fortress is within our reach.
The seagulls are squawking, in a feathery fuss,
As we build our kingdom on that big ol' bus.

Shells line the shore like treasures unclaimed,
But watch for the crabs, they're crafty and claimed!
Their pincers are ready, with twinkles in eyes,
So we barter in giggles, like wise little spies.

As the tide rolls in, we chase all the waves,
Singing off-key like quirky little knaves.
The sun's our spotlight, the sea's our stage,
In this comedy show, we're all the rage!

With shells as our microphones, we belt out the tunes,
While barnacles gather, like rocking raccoons.
We're the stars of this shore, eternal and free,
In this humorous slice of our great jubilee.

Ripples of Change in Tranquil Waters

The river chuckles, with bubbles of glee,
As we dip our toes, just you and me.
Frogs sit serenely, fixing their ties,
While turtles do yoga under cloudy skies.

With each little splash, we stir up some fun,
Creating a ruckus in the glow of the sun.
A fish winks slyly, giving a nod,
In this watery world, he's quite the odd prod.

So let's sail paper boats with wishes and dreams,
As ducks quack away with their befuddled themes.
The gentle waves whisper tales of the past,
Where each little ripple is made to last.

In these tranquil waters, where humor is found,
We dip our souls deep, and joy knows no bounds.
So come, let us laugh with the tide at our feet,
In this swirling adventure, life's whimsical beat.

Sunkissed Echoes of Elation

The sun wore shades, all cool and bright,
While seagulls danced, in pure delight.
Crabs in tuxedos strutted by,
With top hats on, oh my, oh my!

Sandcastles stood, so proud and tall,
Until a wave came with a call.
'Excuse me, sir, your moat is due!'
And poof! It washed away—who knew?

Flip-flops flying, laughter loud,
Tickled toes beneath the crowd.
A beach ball bounces, flies up high,
Like wishes tossed upon the sky.

With each splash, a giggle found,
As jellyfish danced, no worries around.
The waves smiled wide, like silly jest,
In this sunny realm, we're all at our best!

Serenity's Alluring Call

In a hammock strung between two trees,
Lies a sleepy cat, purring with ease.
She dreams of fish, of swimming fins,
While a dog nearby plots joyful spins.

Umbrellas bright, in colors bold,
Block the sun's heat, or so I'm told.
But instead, they twirl in breezy glee,
Like octopus dances, wild and free!

Chairs are scooting to get some shade,
While soda cans seem to invade.
'Pop!' goes one with a fizzy cheer,
The laughter rolls, oh dear, oh dear!

As sunset whispers a cheeky tease,
The stars pop out, like mischievous bees.
Even the moon gives a wink or two,
And we all giggle at this evening view.

Pathways of the Wandering Wave

A lost flip-flop bobbing in the sea,
Searching for its friend, can't you see?
It calls to shells, 'Hey, have you heard?'
The answer is silence, not one chirped!

Crabby confessions fill the air,
As turtles whisper, 'Life's unfair!'
With surfboards washed upon the shore,
They ponder, 'Are we meant for more?'

With ice cream cones, and sticky fingers,
Each joyful bite, a sweet joy lingers.
Seagulls swoop down, oh what a catch,
'Is that mine?' 'No, yours!' in this happy match.

Down the beach, we fleet-footed roam,
Making mischief far from home.
In fences made of driftwood smiles,
We build our dreams in silly styles!

Enchantment at Twilight's Cove

As the sun dips low, the skies ignite,
Mermaids giggle, oh what a sight!
They splash and twirl in colors bold,
With whispered secrets, legends told.

Footprints in sand sing a song,
'It's time for fun; you can't be wrong!'
A starfish tumbles with a grin,
'Come join the dance, you're late! Get in!'

Glowworms twinkle, like fairy lights,
As laughter echoes through the nights.
Driftwood logs become thrones anew,
For kings of silliness, brave and true.

With each wave, joy skips along,
And tides compose a silly song.
In this enchanted, starlit show,
We bask in fun—oh, let it flow!

Balmy Breezes of Possibility

The sun's a giant barbecue,
Grilling dreams with mustard too.
Seagulls squawk in sarcastic tones,
While sandcastles turn into cones.

Flip-flops dance in the warm, soft breeze,
As beach balls float like jellyfish cheese.
Fried fish argue with taco carts,
Napping sunbathers steal hearts.

Juicy jokes from old palm trees,
Whisper secrets in the salty breeze.
A crab in shades does a funny jig,
While kids chase waves and a fat sea pig.

Laughter echoes along the shore,
Where sunscreen wars are never a bore.
Each wave's a giggle, each tide a tease,
In this realm of fun, we find our peace.

Horizons Unfolding Beneath Starlight

The stars above throw a cosmic bash,
Aliens bring snacks; they say, 'Let's clash!'
Dancing comets in hula skirts,
While moonbeams laugh with twinkling flirts.

Plans for a rocket made of cheese,
Shooting for planets with lovely breeze.
Martians swing with Earthlings' style,
And time-travelers forget the mile.

Old constellations tell silly tales,
Of lost socks in celestial gales.
While meteors zoom with a big 'whoosh',
Painting the night with a vibrant swoosh.

In this cosmic laughter, dreams align,
As space-time bends and humor shines.
Far beyond the realm of night,
Joy and nonsense take their flight.

Serenity at the Edge of Dreams

A cotton candy cloud floats by,
Whispers of laughter in the sky.
Dreamers craft wishes with sticky hands,
As the moon plays hopscotch on silver sands.

Unicorns trotting in flip-flops bright,
Chasing marshmallows with all their might.
Dreamscapes filled with giggles galore,
Jellybean rivers forevermore.

Rainbows draped like cozy chit-chat,
As teddy bears share a giggly spat.
Over pillows, soft clouds sail high,
Laughter rolls like waves, oh my!

Finding joy in the strangest places,
In snoozy dreams and funny faces.
At the edge where giggles teem,
We bask in the glow of every dream.

Windswept Visions of Paradise

Kites are tangled in fishermen's nets,
Fish tell tales of flashy regrets.
Mermaids giggle while sipping tea,
In a sea of jokes, come swim with me.

Palm trees doing a silly sway,
As seashells join in for the play.
Seagulls steal fries with crafty flair,
While beach umbrellas are dancing in pairs.

Sandmen built with mismatched toes,
Laughing at waves that dance and pose.
Turtles participating in a race,
With beach balls rolling all over the place.

Joy and whimsy in sandy hues,
Where laughter floats like ocean views.
In this paradise where chuckles reside,
Every wave holds a funny surprise.

Fragments of a Distant Dream

I saw a cat in a sailor's hat,
He danced on sand like a well-fed brat.
A seagull squawked with a funny tone,
Claiming the beach as its own throne.

A crab called out, "Hey, watch your toes!"
As the tide tickled with playful flows.
Shells were like treasures, with prices too high,
I bartered with laughter, oh my, oh my!

The sun wore shades, looking quite cool,
While beach balls bounced like a silly fool.
"Life's a party," shouted a fish with flair,
Waving its fins in the salty air.

As night crept in with a wink and a grin,
We danced with shadows, let the fun begin.
With dreams as sweet as a cold scoop of cream,
We laughed and played—oh, what a dream!

An Odyssey to the Water's Embrace

A duck in a tie quacked at the sun,
Claiming he was the wise, number one.
The waves giggled, tickling my feet,
As I struggled to stand, oh, what a feat!

My rubber ducky, a brave little chap,
Set sail on a wave, looking for a nap.
Seagulls laughed, dropping seaweed jokes,
While I tripped over my own sunburnt cloaks.

I built a grand castle of feathery sand,
But it crumbled down at the touch of my hand.
The tide rolled in with a gentle tease,
Saying, "Next time, my friend, try with ease!"

As dusk painted skies with colors so bright,
I wave goodbye to this whimsical night.
With laughter resounding, I danced with glee,
In this odyssey, oh so carefree!

Glistening Hopes Adrift

A jellyfish jiggled in a neon suit,
It boogied and wiggled, oh what a hoot!
I waved to the starfish, all lined in a row,
They flipped me the fin, putting on a show.

A dolphin appeared, cracking a grin,
"Join me for a swim, come on in!"
But I belly-flopped into the frothy spray,
Making waves of laughter, hip-hip-hooray!

Kites in the sky were all tangled and twisted,
With hopes that soared, none ever listed.
A crab yelled, "Guys, let's not be lame,
Join the fun—this isn't a game!"

As night fell softly with twinkling stars,
We danced on the shore, ignoring our cars.
With glistening hopes and laughter so loud,
We sailed off in dreams, a merry crowd!

Pilgrimage to Joyous Shores

An otter in shades surfed with great flair,
Doing flips and dives, creating wild air.
I sat on the sand, snacks piled too high,
Eating chips while the frisbees flew by.

"Hey there, buddy!" a clam cheekily spoke,
"Don't eat that potato chip, it's a hoax!"
But I shrugged and chomped, living my quest,
For crusaders of chips, we pass the test.

The lighthouse giggled, its light shining bright,
As crabs formed a conga line, oh what a sight!
Surfboards and laughter danced in the tide,
In this joyous pilgrimage, I couldn't hide.

As stars twinkled over the shimmering sea,
I found all the joy that could ever be.
With friends by my side, laughter galore,
We embraced the magic forevermore!

Chasing Horizons with Outstretched Hands

With every stride, we leap and bound,
In this sandy playground, joy is found.
Seagulls squawk, they swoop and dive,
While we compete to be the loudest alive.

Our kites are stuck, on the boardwalk's end,
Tangled in laughter, we cannot pretend.
A gust of wind sends hats a-flying,
As we chase the horizon, collapsing, crying.

The sun's a chef, cooking rays on our skin,
Grilling the day, a delightful din.
We feast on ice cream, the flavors collide,
But sticky fingers— oh, where can we hide?

With footprints trailing, we dance in the sand,
Creating a masterpiece, all unplanned.
As waves clap back, we shiver and play,
Chasing horizons, we'll never delay.

A Journey to the Serene Unknown

We packed our dreams in a roly-poly cart,
Discovering treasures that tickle the heart.
A map made of jelly, a compass of cheers,
Who knew adventures come with such jeers?

In forests of giggles, we wander in bliss,
Trading paths for puddles, who could resist?
With splashes so grand, we sail on a stream,
A journey so silly, it feels like a dream.

The stars are our guides with a wink and a blink,
As laughter erupts, we all start to sink.
Not just in the water, but into our glee,
In the serene unknown, we're wild and free.

Finally, we find a land made of cake,
Where rivers run chocolate, oh, what a mistake!
We'll feast 'til we wobble, and giggle at fate,
In a world made of sweetness, it's never too late.

Rustling Leaves of Reverence

In a forest of giggles, leaves laugh and sway,
Their whispers of nonsense lead us astray.
A tree starts a debate, with a squirrel as judge,
The acorns are frantic, they're ready to budge.

Beneath rustling crowns, we tangle our feet,
With vines full of puns, this nonsense is sweet.
A mushroom is grinning, it joins in our jest,
While pine cones are tossing insults, at best.

The sun playfully pokes through branches above,
As shadows do pirouettes, filled with love.
We bask in the silliness of nature's own tune,
And dance with the bunnies, by the light of the moon.

So here's to the forest, its chuckles and cheer,
With rustling leaves that bring laughter near.
In a world full of whimsy, we find our way,
Celebrating together, come join in the play.

Mysteries Whispered by Gentle Waves

The ocean's a gossip, with secrets to share,
As waves tap the shore, all full of hot air.
They tell of lost castles and mermaids at tea,
And a fish who once swam with a grand bumblebee.

On the beach, we sit, with our toes in the foam,
Building sand towers, our wondrous new home.
But a rogue wave approaches, with a mischievous grin,
In a splash of confusion, we're tossed in a spin.

Our buckets and shovels now float out to sea,
As we chase after treasures, not quite meant to be.
A crab gives a wave, like we're all comrades,
While seagulls roll laughter, in their feathered fads.

With the sun setting low, kissing day goodbye,
The ocean still whispers, no need to be shy.
We'll laugh at the stories the waves bring anew,
As mysteries tumble, all silly but true.

Dreams of Serene Horizons

In lands where llamas wear hats,
And jellybeans grow on trees,
Mermaids trade in funny chats,
While seagulls dance in the breeze.

The sun's a giant slice of cake,
With frosting clouds drifting near,
And every wave a rubber snake,
That tickles toes, brings cheer.

When fish wear shoes, and whales hum tunes,
We skip along the sandy path,
With floating balloons and paper moons,
We laugh off every silly math.

In dreamlands bright where giggles reign,
We find our joy, no need to frown,
With every ray a playful strain,
We dance like clowns, and never drown.

Whispers of Celestial Sands

Beneath the stars, the crabs do juggle,
While sandcastles sprout legs to roam,
The moon spills laughs, but not a struggle,
As we all tumble without a home.

Eagles wear glasses, oh what a sight,
As dolphins argue over who can dive,
With comical fish that puff with fright,
In this vast beach, we come alive.

The breeze carries jokes on a flowing tide,
With waves that tease and tickle toes,
Every grain of sand a little joyride,
Life's absurd, but everyone knows.

So let us frolic like silly geese,
With laughter framed in twilight hues,
Ceaseless fun, and a sprinkle of peace,
In this whimsical place we choose.

Beyond the Glistening Waves

The gulls are plotting a surprise show,
With pies that fly in loop-de-loops,
And upside-down quokkas in a row,
They sing of frolic, twist, and whoops!

Each wave a giggle, each splash a cheer,
As fishes tease with their funny prance,
We lose ourselves in joy sincere,
And join in nature's comic dance.

The tide brings whispers of silly dreams,
Where stars wear hats and sprout pink tails,
Each grain a tale woven with gleams,
Of laughter that never fails.

In sails adorned with wacky flair,
We drift along on giddy streams,
With every turn, we find fresh air,
And swell our souls with laughter themes.

Fragments of Paradise Found

In frothy foam, we fashion crowns,
While crabs don't mind a little prance,
Here, seaweed wears the silliest gowns,
    As we join in the ocean's dance.

Lost socks gather for a parade,
On shores where flip-flops find their friends,
With every wave, new jokes are made,
    As giggles stretch, no bounds nor ends.

The day glows bright, yet puns take flight,
With shells that whisper "come and play,"
    In this odd realm of sheer delight,
    We trade our cares, and just sway.

So here's to life, a grand charade,
With joy as deep as ocean's blue,
In fragments rich, our hearts upgraded,
    In every laugh, we start anew.

A Canvas Painted with Hope

In a land where colors clash,
They paint their dreams with a splash.
Brush strokes dance and twirl about,
Creating smiles, never doubt.

With polka dots and stripes so bright,
They argue over blue and white.
A paint fight turns into a game,
Their canvas grows, just not the same.

The sun dips low, they sip their tea,
With laughter echoing, oh so free.
Each brush a joke, each stroke a pun,
In this wild world, they're never done.

So raise a cup to those who dare,
To splash their hopes beyond compare.
In every laugh, a vivid scene,
A canvas blooms where hope is keen.

Seashells of the Soul

They wander by the sandy shore,
Collecting seashells, oh so lore.
Each one tells a tale so neat,
Of ocean whispers and salty feet.

With every crack and every line,
They find a tale that's truly divine.
A shell, a shoe, who can really tell?
Fashion revealed, they ring the bell.

They giggle as they polish bright,
Each seashell sparkles in the light.
An octopus joins in for the fun,
Wearing shells, claiming he's the one.

So gather 'round, the sea's embrace,
In every shell, a smiling face.
With laughter shared and stories bold,
Their treasure trove, a song retold.

Embracing the Light Beyond Bounds

They chase the sun with silly hats,
Dancing in circles, like happy rats.
Shadows laugh and join the spree,
As light reveals their glee-filled glee.

Hot air balloons and kite-flying jest,
The wind whispers tales of the best.
Up in the sky, they reach for stars,
Dreaming of journeys to planets, Mars.

With giggles shared beneath the rays,
They plot antics for daring plays.
A game of tag where stars align,
Each moment bright, distinctly divine.

So here they roam, beyond the crowds,
Embracing hope, laughing out loud.
In every spark where laughter's found,
They dance forever, joy unbound.

Lighthouses of Longing and Lore

Waves crash, a giggle fills the air,
A lighthouse stands, with quirky flair.
Its light a beacon, flashing glee,
Guiding sailors, or so they see.

The keeper's hat, it's far too wide,
He juggles lanterns with great pride.
A seagull swoops and steals his snack,
As laughter echoes, there's no lack.

The stories spill from lantern light,
Of ships that danced through day and night.
With tales of love and pirates bold,
They paint the sea in hues of gold.

So gather 'round, let laughter reign,
In tales of lighthouses, never plain.
With each flicker, they find delight,
In shipping dreams across the night.

Celestial Paths Through Gentle Clouds

Balloons float up, chasing the moon,
Squirrels dance to a cheeky tune.
Stars wink at us from dusty skies,
While llamas wear their grand disguise.

Kites tussle with the zephyr's cheer,
As giggles echo, drawing near.
Pies bake with a comical craze,
Their crusts are lost in sugary haze.

Umbrellas sprout like mushrooms bright,
Dancing divas at twilight's light.
Clouds do cartwheels, fluffy and spry,
As the sun tips its hat to the sky.

In this realm of laughter and fun,
Where socks and sandals frolic and run.
We chase the tickles of time on a road,
With silly hats, we lighten our load.

A Sanctuary Beyond the Ordinary

In a town where cats play chess,
Every dog wears a fancy dress.
Houses wobble on stilts of dreams,
As laughter bubbles in sunny streams.

Bicycles dance without a care,
With rosy cheeks and windswept hair.
Coffee cups wear mustaches bold,
And stories of mischief unfold.

Fluffy pillows tumble and roll,
While kooky fish swim with a goal.
Garden gnomes break into song,
As trees sway and hum along.

Here, the ordinary takes a twist,
In the land of giggles, who could resist?
With every corner, a surprise to greet,
Where the mundane and the magical meet.

Radiance Found in Everyday Moments

A spoon sings sweetly while stirring stew,
While slippers on cats do a waltz or two.
Curtains thrash with a breeze so bold,
As socks tumble out, their colors uncontrolled.

Chairs gossip as they rock with glee,
While the clock ticks to the beat of tea.
Jellybeans spill like a rainbow's dream,
Transforming the floor into a sweet theme.

Lamps wink back with a friendly glow,
As frogs hop in a polka dot row.
Every moment, a source of delight,
In the quirkiest corners, life feels right.

Where laughter bubbles in every crack,
And even dust bunnies join the flack.
In these rich moments, joy will bloom,
Where the mundane bursts with color and room.

The Waves That Lull the Heart's Yearning

Splashing sailors on a quest for snacks,
While seagulls wear outrageous hats.
Waves whisper secrets in playful tones,
As fish throw parties with laughter and moans.

Crabs hold hands in a conga line,
Beneath the sun, they sip on brine.
Surfboards dance with a graceful flair,
As jellyfish glide without a care.

Driftwood sits like a wise old sage,
Spouting wisdom from a light-hearted page.
Sandcastles glow with silly pride,
While the tide giggles and tries to bide.

Every splash is a song once sung,
In this kingdom where childhood's flung.
As waves curl up with laughter clear,
The heart's longing finds joy right here.

Portals to Enchanted Realities

A door swings wide with a creaky sound,
In a land where lost socks are always found.
Cats in top hats sip tea and croon,
While fish in tuxedos dance to a tune.

Marshmallow mountains that grow with delight,
Where unicorns argue about who flies right.
A snail on a skateboard zooms past in haste,
As a wizard with ice cream shares a sweet taste.

Balloons talk loudly, gossiping with flair,
While jellybeans juggle in midair.
A giant giraffe plays hopscotch, oh my!
In this world, we just laugh and sigh.

Dreams sprout wings, take flight like a kite,
Each adventure twisting with silly delight.
Join the parade that's not bound by fate,
In this merry realm, we're never late!

Stargazing by the Glimmering Tide

Stars wink and giggle as they take their place,
While the moon plays hide-and-seek with grace.
Crabs recite poetry on their tiny stage,
As dolphins perform antics, drawing a page.

The ocean sings softly, a lullaby sweet,
While sand castles crumble with laughter replete.
A fish wearing glasses reads books on the shore,
Then jumps through the waves to demand encore.

With each wave that crashes, a joke takes a dive,
Barnacles whisper, keeping the beach alive.
We stargaze with snacks as the night takes its form,
In the midst of these giggles, we weather the storm.

As sand tickles toes and cool breezes blow,
We laugh at the antics of the moon's ethereal glow.
Stars share their secrets, while the sea takes a bow,
In this dance of the night, we all take a vow!

The Promise of Tomorrow's Sky

Kites made of dreams flutter high in the air,
As jellyfish jump rope without a care.
Rainbows giggle as they twist in the light,
While clouds wear pajamas and dance half the night.

Tomorrow's horizon is painted with cheer,
Whispers of wonders that tickle the ear.
A potato sings opera from the garden fair,
While squirrels in tuxedos do steps in the square.

The sun sneezes glitter on all that it sees,
And butterflies moo, surprising the bees.
With each dawn that breaks, new antics unfold,
As laughter erupts in colors bold.

A promise of whimsy floats high in the sky,
Where dreams come alive with a jubilant sigh.
Join in the fun, don't let the day fade,
In this fanciful dance, we're unafraid!

Navigating the Waters of Wonder

A boat made of marshmallows sails through the mist,
With a captain who's always forgetting his list.
Oars carved from candy that shimmer and shine,
As fish in bow ties grace every line.

The waves whisper secrets beneath the hull's pluck,
While pies in the sky rain down bits of luck.
A parrot in spectacles gives navigational tips,
While the crew juggles donuts and does silly flips.

Each twist in the current brings laughter anew,
As an octopus plays the accordion too.
The wind carries giggles that dance on the sea,
In this joyful adventure, it's just you and me.

We'll sail through the laughter, we'll bask in the play,
With a map made of wishes to brighten our day.
In the waters of wonder, let's drift ever free,
As the world spins around us, just you and me!

Whispers of Enchanted Tides

The waves giggle, a playful sound,
As clams exchange secrets from underground.
Seagulls in top hats dance by the shore,
While crabs in sunglasses shout, "More! More!"

A starfish strumming a tiny guitar,
Sings to the fish, who crowd from afar.
With jellyfish waltzing, they float and sway,
Bubbles pop-laughing, come join the play!

The sun does a limbo, shining bright,
Merging colors in a whimsical flight.
Shells wear a grin, adorned with delight,
As coconut cocktails flow through the night!

In this sandy realm of frolic and cheer,
Life is a party, no need for a steer.
With laughter and fun, we dance like the breeze,
Join the tide's romp; let's do as we please!

The Horizon's Gentle Caress

A horizon that's painted in silly hues,
Where turtles juggle their best, brightest shoes.
Laughter erupts from the crabs in a race,
As they trip on their shells, what a funny place!

The ocean does stand-up, a comedic splash,
With fish-tales that tickle and make us all gasp.
Seashells roll over, they're laughing in heaps,
While octopuses practice their dance with the beats.

A cheeky parrot, with jokes galore,
Tells tales of the sailors from days of yore.
The wind tickles kites, flying high in the sky,
Over waves that giggle, as they whisper why!

Gather 'round all, in this carnival scene,
Where the whimsical waters can seldom be mean.
With wisps of delight and a sprinkle of cheer,
Belly-laughs echo and bring joy all year!

Cornucopia of Vibrant Shores

A beach where the sand is a canvas of cheer,
With fruits growing wild and a pie-picking peer.
Coconuts wiggle and roll down the way,
While bananas tango in bright, sunny ballet.

The seaweed's a jester, cracking wise jokes,
As dolphins wear bowties and swig fizzy cokes.
There's fruit punch in shells, with umbrellas on top,
While the sun tells the waves, "I'll never stop!"

Tides serve up laughter, a feast we adore,
With sky-high custard and giggle galore.
Crabs host a party with music and fun,
When the stars start to twinkle, the laughter's not done!

So gather your friends; join the mix and the jig,
In a world of whimsy, where all do a gig.
With every sweet wave that tickles the shore,
Join this lush banquet, who could ask for more?

Journeys to a Timeless Eden

In a paradise where the sun likes to play,
Fish wear top hats and dance all day.
With turtles telling tales in curious ways,
Time ticks in chuckles, delighting our stays.

Breezes blow softly, like whispers of joy,
As a clam plays the drums—what a clever boy!
The clouds roll in with a giggle and swirl,
As sea stars twinkle and freely unfurl.

A picnic of laughter laid out on the sand,
With snacks from the ocean, uniquely unplanned.
For mermaids and whales join the bash with a cheer,
As fun sails the tides, bringing smiles and good cheer.

So pack up your dreams, come join the parade,
In this timeless Eden, let memories invade.
With silliness reigning, this journey's like play,
On shores of pure joy, let our hearts lead the way!

Tales from the Edge of Eden

In paradise, a monkey stole my hat,
He swung from trees, all cheeky and fat.
I chased him down, but he laughed with glee,
"This is best hat! Just wait and see!"

A talking fish offered me a drink,
It winked and laughed; I began to think.
"Just one sip!" it said with a grin,
Next thing I knew, I was swimming in sin!

A cactus wearing glasses read my book,
Its prickly wisdom? Not worth a look.
"Dude, just chill! Embrace the blight!"
I smiled back, then ran from its sight.

In this wild land, oddities roam,
Every step feels oddly like home.
So come along, let's laugh and play,
At the edge of Eden, we'll seize the day!

Canvas of a Distant Dream

I painted clouds with cotton candy fluff,
The sun turned purple; it was rather tough.
A rabbit critiqued from his pastel chair,
"You call that art? You need some flair!"

With brushes made of gummy worms,
I sketched out worlds with comical swirls.
A fish in a beret said, "Well done!"
Then dove right in for more artistic fun!

The trees burst into song, quite out of tune,
They wobbled and jiggled under the moon.
A squirrel with flair held a wild dance,
Inviting us all to take a chance!

In this whimsical realm where dreams unite,
Imagination takes off, taking flight.
So paint your world in wacky hues,
In this canvas, nothing's to lose!

Odes to the Luminous Abyss

A glowing jellyfish wrote me a poem,
It flowed with grace, like a swirling chrome.
"Dear friend, don't fear the ebb and flow,"
It giggled, as it put on a show.

A crab in a tux went out for a stroll,
It danced with shells, playing a role.
"Why so serious? Just loosen up!"
It winked and spun with a floppy cup.

The seaweed sang of underwater fame,
Each wave applauded, never felt shame.
A clam, it belted out a big high note,
Made all the fishies simply gloat!

In this glimmering place, laughter thrives,
Even deep down, the humor drives.
So dive right in, let the fun ensue,
In the luminous depths, it's all for you!

Secrets Written in the Sand

I found a message scribbled by the shore,
It read, "Don't feed the crabs! They want more!"
A sign next to it claimed, 'Danger ahead!'
Turns out, it was just a crab drawing bread!

The tide brought treasures, shiny and bright,
A broken flip-flop had won the fight.
"Wear me!" it squeaked, "I'm quite the catch!"
But I walked away, saying, "You're a match!"

A seagull squawked, demanding my fries,
It swooped down low, oh such surprise!
"You can't hide food from one so sly,
Hand them over, or else I'll cry!"

In the grains of sand, stories unfold,
Of silly antics and laughter untold.
So come, my friend, and join the fun,
In this sandy world, we're never done!

The Promise of Golden Beaches

Sunbathers wear hats shaped like cake,
Swim trunks that rattle with every shake.
Seagulls debate a sandwich prize,
While sunscreen drips from noses, oh my!

Beach balls bounce, and laughter flows,
A crab with sunglasses strikes a pose.
Towels like flags in wild disarray,
As sunscreen steers dreams far away.

Sandcastles rise, a mystical scene,
With moats that shimmer like jellybeans.
A kid screams, 'Look! I caught a wave!'
But all he caught was a smelly grave.

As sunset paints the sky in gold,
A tale of beach flips as it's told.
We leave with sandy feet and cheer,
For fun's the treasure we hold dear.

Reflections in the Tranquil Tide

Mirror-like water, a fishy grin,
Splashing about in a watery din.
Flip-flops that squeak and sandals that squeal,
In a tidepool's depth, we hunt for a meal.

Turtles in shades take a lazy stroll,
While jellyfish dance like they've lost control.
An otter winks, sloshing through grace,
As crabs hustle sideways in a racing pace.

Mats filled with snacks, we lay in the sun,
With chips that compete, 'Can you eat just one?'
Splashing with friends, the sea's a delight,
Until someone falls and 'splashes' the night.

Reflections of giggles, the tides keep the score,
We laugh till it hurts, and then laugh some more.
As waves come and go, we cherish the tide,
Finding joy in the chaos, where laughter resides.

Chasing the Horizon's Glow

Kites soar high, colored like sprinkles,
Chasing the sun as it winks and twinkles.
Skateboards zoom as we weave through the air,
With wind whipped hair and not a single care.

Pies flying past, what's that in the sky?
Is it cake or a drone? Oh my, oh my!
The horizon giggles, teasing our fate,
As we chase after dreams, not wanting to wait.

A dog steals a sandwich, bolts down the lane,
While seagulls unite in a feathery train.
We run with abandon, lost in the chase,
With laughter igniting the bright, open space.

At dusk, the horizon shares a warm wink,
We gather our stories, together we think.
What a day it's been—full of whimsical lore,
Chasing the glow, who could ask for more?

Serenade of the Wistful Wind

The wind hums a tune, so breezy and spry,
Whistling through beach huts with a curious sigh.
Flip-flops engage in a tap dance routine,
While beach umbrellas flap like they're mean.

A sunburnt octopus, hiding away,
Winks at the gulls, is he here to stay?
The sand sings a lullaby, gritty and sweet,
As kids wade right in, with splashes of feet.

Windsurfers try, but tumble and flip,
Flying through the air like a wayward chip.
Seashells gossip, 'Did you see that fall?'
The wind just chuckles, 'That's the sport of it all!'

As day dips low, the breezy serenade,
Clutches our hearts, in this laughing parade.
With grains in our toes and hearts open wide,
We dance in the breeze—oh, what a ride!

www.ingramcontent.com/pod-product-compliance
Lightning Source LLC
Chambersburg PA
CBHW072119070526
44585CB00016B/1506